FAVOURITE
HALLOWEEN
AND BONFIRE NIGHT
RECIPES

Compiled by Simon Haseltine

Illustrated by Helen Poole

SALMON

Index

Apple, Pumpkin and Cinnamon Crumble 27
Beastly Burgers 10
Blood Red Cabbage 26
Bonfire Apple and Cinnamon Pasties 6
Bonfire Hash 13
Bonfire Toffee 44
Butternut and Tomato Lasagne 14
Catherine Wheel Pizzas 21
Cheesy Scones 40
Chilli Veggie Burgers 15
Chocolate Chip Cookie Caterpillar 43
Curried Pumpkin Soup 23
Easy Peanut Brittle 37
Ghostly Graveyard Trifle 29
Ghouly Goulash Soup 24
Haunted Cottage Pie 16
Hot Chicken Wings 10
Jack-O-Lantern Pie 5
Lamb and Pumpkin Curry 11
Liquorice Ice Cream 30

Meringue Ghosts 31
Mulled Cider 46
Old Fashioned Apple Pie 34
Pumpkin Damper 45
Pumpkin Lasagne 18
Pumpkin Pie 8
Pumpkin Stew 3
Rocket Fuel *(Bloody Mary)* 47
Scary Sandwiches 22
Spooky Hot Dog Bugs 7
Spooky Pancakes 30
Sticky Bonfire Pudding 32
Toffee Apples 38
Triple Chocolate Brownies 37
Venison Stew 19
Warming Hot Chocolate 46
Warming Whisky Baked Apples 35
Witches Hats 42
Witches Slices 39
Worm Brew *(Non Alcholic Bloody Mary)* 47

Printed and Published by J. Salmon Ltd., Sevenoaks, England © Copyright

Pumpkin Stew

2 onions (peeled and chopped)
2 carrots (peeled and chopped)
2 sticks celery (chopped)
Oil
2 bay leaves
Pinch dried mixed herbs

1 teaspoon smoked paprika
2 cloves garlic (crushed)
100g soup mix pulses
Large pumpkin (peeled and chopped)
2 eating apples (peeled and chopped)
1.5 ltrs vegetable stock

Sauté the onion, carrot and celery in a little oil for 10 minutes until softened. Add the bay leaves, mixed herbs, paprika and garlic and stir for a few more minutes. Transfer to a slow cooker and then add the pulses, pumpkin and apples. Pour over the stock (enough to just cover the vegetables) and cook on a low setting for around 4 hours. Serve with a jacket potato and a dollop of sour cream. Serves 6.

Jack-O-Lantern Pie

1 onion (peeled and chopped)   Oil
500g minced beef   420g tin baked beans
400g tin chopped tomatoes   Dash chilli sauce (to taste)
Pinch dried mixed herbs   1 tin sweetcorn
Gravy granules (to thicken)
Shortcrust pastry – enough for one pie topping
1 egg (yolk only)   Yellow food colouring

Preheat the oven to 230°C/450°F/Gas 8. Sauté the chopped onion in a little oil for 5 minutes until softened then add the minced beef and brown for a further 10 minutes. Add the baked beans, chopped tomatoes, chilli sauce and mixed herbs and stir until heated through. Next, add the sweetcorn and simmer for 20 minutes, then add a little water and some gravy granules and stir for a further 10 minutes to thicken. Meanwhile, roll out the pastry large enough to fit a medium-sized dish. With a sharp knife, cut out a jack-o-lantern face, using the leftover pieces to decorate the hair and face – use a little water to secure in place. Whisk the egg yolk with a little of the yellow food colouring and brush over the pastry face. Ladle the minced beef pie filling into the pie dish, top with the pastry face and bake in the oven for 10 to 15 minutes until golden brown. Serve with mashed potatoes. Serves 4.

Bonfire Apple and Cinnamon Pasties

4 cooking apples (peeled, cored and chopped)   Splash lemon juice
50g demerara sugar   1 teaspoon ground cinnamon
Pinch ground ginger   3 sheets puff pastry (thawed and rolled)
1 egg (beaten)   50g caster sugar (for sprinkling)
Ground cinnamon (for sprinkling)

Preheat the oven to 200°C/400°F/Gas 6. Prepare the apples and sprinkle with the lemon juice. Gently cook the apples in a saucepan for around 10 minutes until they start to soften. Add the demerara sugar and spices and continue to cook for a further 5 minutes until the apples are tender, then allow to cool. Meanwhile, cut 4 rounds from each puff pastry sheet using a 10cm pastry cutter. Place a good dollop of apple mixture on one half of each round, then fold over to enclose the filling, wetting and pressing the edges to seal. Place the pasties on a greased baking tray, brush with the egg and bake in the oven for around 25 minutes until golden brown. Remove from the oven and immediately dust the pasties with caster sugar and a little cinnamon. Serve hot or cold. Makes 12 pasties.

Spooky Hot Dog Bugs

1 pack frozen puff pastry (thawed)
24 sausages
1 bag potato chips (long hard ones)
Thick tomato ketchup
American mustard (squeezy bottle)

Preheat the oven to 190°C/375°F/Gas 5. Roll out the puff pastry and cut into 24 rectangles, each large enough to wrap around a sausage to create a sausage roll. Once rolled, pinch the seam to seal. Place seam-side down onto a greased baking tray and bake for around 15 minutes or until golden brown. Remove from the oven and insert the potato chips into the lower sides of the pastry to create bugs with 6 legs. Place two in the top of one end for antennae. Decorate the backs of each bug with alternate stripes of tomato ketchup and mustard, then make 2 eyes with drops of ketchup on the end of the sausage roll below the antennae, to create a face. Serve jumbled on a plate warm or cold. Makes 24 hot dog bugs.

Pumpkin Pie

Medium pumpkin (peeled and finely chopped)
2 eggs plus 1 yolk
75g soft dark brown sugar
2 teaspoons allspice
275ml double cream
1 sweet shortcrust pastry case (22cm)
Foil

Preheat the oven to 200°C/400°F/Gas 6. Place the pumpkin on a baking tray, cover with foil and roast in the oven for 30 minutes or until tender. Allow to cool slightly, then press through a coarse sieve. Set aside to cool before blending in a food processor to a purée. Break the eggs into a large bowl and whisk. Place the sugar, spice and cream in a pan and bring to a gentle simmer, then immediately pour over the eggs and whisk. Next, add the pumpkin purée, still whisking to combine everything thoroughly. Reduce the oven temperature to 180°C/350°F/Gas 4. Pour the filling into the pastry case and bake for 40 minutes or until cooked but still slightly wobbly in the centre. Serve warm with a dollop of whipped cream. Serves 6.

Beastly Burgers

4 beef burgers   4 burger buns   8 squares burger cheese
2 large pickled gherkins (sliced)   Tomato ketchup

Fry the beef burgers until cooked through, then place one on the base of each bun. Cut the burger cheese into 24 triangles in total (use more squares if required). Place the triangles above and below each burger to form fang-like teeth hanging downwards outside the bun. Put the top of the bun on each burger and then add 2 slices of gherkin on top of each bun to form eyes. Dot each eye with a single blob of tomato ketchup to complete the effect. Serves 4.

Hot Chicken Wings

24 chicken wings   Oil   1 bottle cayenne hot pepper sauce
250g butter   Several dashes Worcestershire sauce

Preheat the oven to 170°C/325°F/Gas 3. Sauté the chicken wings in oil for around 10 minutes until cooked through, turning a few times. Remove and drain on kitchen paper. Next, in a saucepan, heat the cayenne sauce and butter over medium-low heat. Add the Worcestershire sauce and bring to the boil, then remove from the heat. Place the wings in an ovenproof dish and pour the hot sauce over the top. Toss to coat, and then bake in the oven for 15 minutes. Serves 4 to 6.

Lamb and Pumpkin Curry

2 large onions (peeled and chopped)   Oil
3 cloves garlic (peeled and crushed)   1 teaspoon ground ginger
1 chilli (finely chopped – seeds removed)
350g lamb (cubed)   Large pumpkin (peeled and chopped)
5 tablespoons Balti curry paste
800ml vegetable stock   400ml tin coconut milk
400g tin chopped tomatoes   100g soup mix lentils
Handful coriander leaves

In a large frying pan, sauté the onion in a little oil for 5 minutes until soft. Add the garlic, ginger and chilli and cook for a further few minutes. Next, add the lamb, stir to cover well, and fry over a high heat for 5 minutes until lightly brown on all sides. Add the curry paste and cook for 5 minutes, stirring all the time. Transfer to a slow cooker, add the stock, coconut milk, chopped tomatoes, lentils and pumpkin, then stir and cover. Cook for at least 4 hours. Serve with rice and a sprinkling of coriander leaves. Serves 6.

Bonfire Hash

1 red onion (peeled and chopped)
Oil
500g minced beef
2 tablespoons tomato purée
250ml beef stock
Dash Worcestershire sauce
Salt and pepper (to season)
2 tins baked beans with sausages

Sauté the onion in a little oil for 5 minutes until softened, then add the minced beef and fry for 10 minutes until brown. Add the tomato purée, stock, Worcestershire sauce and a little salt and pepper then simmer for 30 minutes, stirring a few times. Add the baked beans and sausages and heat through. Serve with crusty bread. Serves 6.

Butternut and Tomato Lasagne

Oil
1 onion (peeled and chopped)
1 butternut squash (peeled and chopped into small cubes)
Pinch dried mixed herbs
4 cloves garlic (peeled and crushed)
400g tin chopped tomatoes
8 sheets dried lasagne
500ml cheese sauce (homemade or packet)
25g mature Cheddar cheese (grated)

Preheat the oven to 180°C/350°F/Gas 4. Prepare the vegetables, then heat a little oil in a frying pan and sauté the onion and squash for around 10 minutes, until softened. Add the mixed herbs, garlic and chopped tomatoes, stir and simmer for 10 minutes. Next, spoon a quarter of the vegetable mixture into the bottom of a greased ovenproof dish, layer with lasagne sheets, then top with a little cheese sauce. Repeat these layers 3 times finishing with the remaining cheese sauce. Sprinkle the grated cheese over the top. Bake in the oven for around 50 minutes until the cheese topping is golden brown and bubbling. Serve with garlic bread and a green salad. Serves 4.

Chilli Veggie Burgers

Oil   1 onion (peeled and thinly sliced)
2 carrots (peeled and finely chopped)   2 courgettes (finely chopped)
Handful spinach leaves (chopped)   Small tin kidney beans (drained)
1 teaspoon chilli flakes (or less to taste)   Pinch dried mixed herbs
1 heaped tablespoon flour   1 teaspoon mustard powder or dry mustard
1 egg (beaten)   Burger buns

Heat the oil in a frying pan and sauté the onion and carrot for 10 minutes or until soft. Add the courgettes and spinach and sauté for a further 5 minutes. Remove to a bowl and leave to cool. Meanwhile, mash the kidney beans then add to the cooled vegetable mixture, together with the chilli flakes, mixed herbs, flour, mustard and egg. Mix well, then chill for 30 minutes before forming into 4 patties. Fry in hot oil for around 10 minutes, turning once, to cook through. Serve in the buns with your favourite ketchup. Makes 4 burgers.

Haunted Cottage Pie

2 onions (peeled and finely chopped)   Oil
500g minced beef   1 beef stock cube (crumbled)
Pinch dried mixed herbs   400g tin chopped tomatoes
1 tin garden peas (retain 12 peas for decoration)
1 tin sweetcorn   Dash Worcestershire sauce
Beef gravy granules (to thicken)
10 medium-sized potatoes   100g grated Cheddar cheese (grated)
Dash milk

Preheat the oven to 190°C/375°F/Gas 5. Sauté the onion in a little oil for 5 minutes until softened, then add the minced beef, stock cube and mixed herbs. Sauté for a further 10 minutes, stirring regularly, until the beef has browned. Add the chopped tomatoes, peas, sweetcorn, Worcestershire sauce and simmer for 20 minutes until cooked through. Add a little water and gravy granules if required to thicken. Meanwhile, simmer the potatoes for around 20 minutes until cooked, drain and mash with the grated cheese and a little milk. Place the beef mixture into a large ovenproof dish, then dollop the potato on top to form 6 upright ghost-like figures – make sure the potato ghosts are evenly spaced for each serving. Place 2 peas into each ghost to form the eyes, then bake in the oven for 20 minutes until just brown. Serves 6.

Pumpkin Lasagne

Large pumpkin (peeled and chopped)   2 red onions (peeled and sliced)
Oil   2 tins (400g each) chopped tomatoes
2 tablespoons smoked paprika (or to taste)
Pinch dried mixed herbs   250g ricotta cheese
Salt and pepper (to season)   8 sheets dried lasagne
350ml cheese sauce (homemade or packet)
25g Cheddar cheese (grated)

Preheat the oven to 180°C/350°F/Gas 4. In a large frying pan, sauté the pumpkin and onion in a little oil for 10 minutes until softened. Add the chopped tomatoes and gently simmer for around an hour until the pumpkin is cooked, adding a little water if required. Next, stir through the paprika, mixed herbs, ricotta cheese and season to taste. Place a layer of lasagne sheets on the base of an ovenproof dish and ladle over a third of the pumpkin mixture. Repeat for 2 more layers of lasagne sheets, finishing with a layer of pumpkin mixture. Pour over the cheese sauce, sprinkle with the grated cheese and bake in the oven for 30 minutes or until golden brown. Serves 4.

Venison Stew

800g venison (cubed)   4 tablespoons flour
Salt and pepper (to season)   Oil
3 red onions (peeled and chopped)   4 carrots (peeled and sliced)
2 sticks celery (sliced)   2 cloves garlic (peeled and crushed)
1 tablespoon juniper berries (crushed)
Pinch dried mixed herbs   1 knob butter
200ml red wine   500g small salad potatoes (cubed)
2 beef stock cubes (crumbled)
Packet cooked chestnuts
3 tablespoons redcurrant jelly
Bunch parsley (chopped)

Pop the venison cubes in a large mixing bowl with half the flour, seasoned with salt and pepper and coat well. Add a little oil to a large pan and fry for 5 minutes or until brown on all sides. Add the onion, carrot, celery, garlic, juniper berries, mixed herbs and the butter, together with the red wine. Stir, then place the lid on and simmer for a further 10 minutes, stirring occasionally. Add the potatoes and stock cubes and enough water to just cover. Bring to the boil, then gently simmer for 2 hours. Remove the lid and add the chestnuts, redcurrant jelly and parsley, plus the remaining flour (premixed with a little water to form a runny paste). Stir and cook for a further 10 minutes or until thickened. Serve hot in large bowls with chunky bread. Serves 6.

Catherine Wheel Pizzas

4 heaped tablespoons tomato purée
4 small pizza bases (single serving size)
Pinch dried mixed herbs
Selection of toppings (pepper, mushrooms, red onion – all finely sliced)
100g mature Cheddar cheese (grated)
Thick tomato ketchup

Preheat the oven to 220°C/425°F/Gas 7 and lightly grease a baking tray. Spread 1 heaped tablespoon of tomato purée over each pizza base, then sprinkle with the mixed herbs. Add a selection of toppings, then top with the grated cheese, ensuring an even covering. Place on the baking tray and bake for 20 minutes or until the cheese is golden brown. Remove from the oven and allow to cool slightly, then pipe a swirl of tomato ketchup over each pizza to create a Catherine wheel effect. Serves 4.

Scary Sandwiches

Butter (softened for spreading)
10 slices white bread
Slices ham and cheese
Slices cucumber and tomatoes
Tomato ketchup, mustard, pickle etc
Ghost, Bat and Witch shaped cookie cutters (or template)
Pomegranate seeds
Radishes (sliced into mouth shapes)

Butter each slice of bread and top with a selection of ham, cheese, cucumber and tomato, then spread with either tomato ketchup, mustard or pickle. With large Ghost, Bat and Witch shaped cookie cutters, cut out the sandwiches. Use the pomegranate seeds to create ghoulish eyes and radish slices for mouths. If you don't have a cutter, draw a ghost, bat and witch's hat shape onto card to create a template you can cut around. Serve with a sprinkling of cress. Makes 10 sandwiches.

Curried Pumpkin Soup

3 onions (peeled and chopped)   1 red chilli (chopped)
1 medium pumpkin (peeled and chopped)
1 teaspoon curry powder (or slightly more to taste)
400g tin chopped tomatoes
500ml vegetable stock   400ml tin coconut milk
Tub sour cream

Place the onion, chilli and pumpkin in a frying pan with a little oil and sauté for around 10 minutes until they begin to soften. Add the curry powder, chopped tomatoes and stock, bring to the boil and gently simmer for 20 minutes or until the pumpkin is cooked. Leave to cool, then blend to a smooth soup. Add the coconut milk and heat through. Ladle into individual bowls and drizzle the sour cream in 3 circles over the soup. With a skewer, draw 6 lines out from the centre to form a spider's web design. Serve hot with a chunk of crusty bread. Serves 4.

Ghouly Goulash Soup

2 onions (peeled and thinly sliced)
2 carrots (peeled and finely chopped)
1 parsnip (peeled and finely chopped)
Oil
3 tablespoons smoked paprika (or slightly less to taste)
2 cloves garlic (peeled and crushed)
3 potatoes (peeled and finely chopped)
2 tins (400g each) chopped tomatoes
1 ltr vegetable stock

Sauté the onion, carrot and parsnip in a little oil for 10 minutes until softened. Add the paprika, garlic, potatoes, chopped tomatoes and stir thoroughly. Pour over the stock, bring to the boil and simmer for 25 minutes or until the vegetables are cooked through. Serve with a dollop of sour cream and crusty bread. Serves 6.

Blood Red Cabbage

4 slices bacon (chopped)
Oil
Half a red cabbage (shredded)
Salt and pepper (to season)
2 green apples (peeled and thinly sliced into strips)
100ml boiling water
1 teaspoon flour
3 tablespoons malt vinegar
1 tablespoon brown sugar

Fry the bacon in a little oil for a few minutes until crisp, then remove from the pan. Add the shredded cabbage to the bacon fat, along with a little salt and pepper. Add the sliced apples and fold through. Sauté for 5 minutes, then pour over the boiling water and gently simmer for 15 minutes until the cabbage has cooked through, stirring regularly. Meanwhile, blend the flour with the vinegar and sugar and add to the cooked cabbage mixture. Heat through for a few minutes, stirring all the time, until thickened. Serve hot as a side dish to a stew or burgers. Serves 4.

Apple, Pumpkin and Cinnamon Crumble

1kg cooking apples (peeled, cored and sliced)
Splash lemon juice   Small pumpkin (peeled and chopped)
Pinch cinnamon   100g demerara sugar
For the crumble topping:
100g butter (softened – plus a little extra)
50g flour   50g porridge oats   150g walnuts (chopped)
Additional demerara sugar (for sprinkling)

Preheat the oven to 180°C/350°F/Gas 4. Prepare the apples and sprinkle with the lemon juice. Place the apple and pumpkin into a saucepan, with a splash of water and gently cook for around 10 minutes until the fruit has softened. Add the cinnamon and sugar and cook for a further 5 minutes. Meanwhile, place the dry topping ingredients in a mixing bowl and rub in the butter, until the mixture resembles breadcrumbs. Place the apple and pumpkin mixture into a buttered ovenproof dish and top with the crumble. Sprinkle over a little additional demerara sugar and bake in the oven for 45 minutes or until golden brown. Serves 6.

Ghostly Graveyard Trifle

1 large strawberry flavoured Swiss roll   2 tins strawberries
2 packets strawberry jelly   500ml custard   1 large tub double cream
1 tablespoon icing sugar   Green food colouring
Icing pen   1 packet Rich Tea 'finger' biscuits   1 bar flaky chocolate
1 packet ghostly Halloween sweets   Edible glittery sprinkles   Sparklers

Freeze the Swiss roll prior to making the trifle, as it will stay firm and won't absorb all the jelly. The day before serving, cut the frozen Swiss roll into slices and layer the base of a large serving bowl. Open the tins of strawberries and drain, saving the liquid. Place the strawberries over and around the Swiss roll slices. Make up the jelly in accordance with the packet instructions but use the reserved strawberry juice in place of cold water. Pour the jelly over the Swiss roll and leave to set overnight. The following morning, make up the custard in accordance with the packet instructions or use ready made and pour over the jelly. Leave to set for a few hours. Prior to serving, whip the cream, icing sugar and green food colouring (around 8 drops) and dollop over the custard to form an uneven grassy graveyard. Using an icing pen, write 'RIP' on the top third of the finger biscuits and place in the cream at jaunty angles to represent old grave stones. Next, crumble the chocolate bar and pile the 'chocolate earth' over each grave to form a hump. Decorate each grave with some scary Halloween sweets. Finally, sprinkle the edible glitter around the cream. When serving, carefully light some sparklers and place in the trifle to create a ghostly, smoky effect. Serves 8.

Spooky Pancakes

Pancake mixture (enough for 8 small pancakes – around 500ml)
1 teaspoon cocoa powder   1 teaspoon sugar   Oil

Make the pancake batter until it is the consistency of single cream. Transfer around 4 tablespoons of the batter mix into a small bowl and add the cocoa powder and sugar, whisking until smooth. Heat a little oil in a small frying pan, dollop 3 blobs of the cocoa batter mix to form 2 eyes and a mouth, around 2cm apart. Fry for about 30 seconds to set, then pour a ladle of batter mix over the face and downwards, finishing with a slight swirl to one side to form a ghost-like figure. Cook for around 90 seconds, then flip the pancake over and cook for a further 1 minute. Remove from the pan, set aside to keep warm then make the remaining pancakes. Serve with golden syrup. Makes 8 spooky pancakes.

Liquorice Ice Cream

4 egg yolks   125g sugar   3 teaspoons raw liquorice powder
1 lemon (grated rind)   500ml whipping cream
Liquorice Allsorts and liquorice ribbons

Whisk the egg yolks and sugar together, then fold in the liquorice powder and grated lemon rind. Whisk the cream until thick, then fold into the egg yolks. Pour the mixture into an ice-cream machine and operate according to the instructions. Serve in individual bowls, decorated with Liquorice Allsorts and liquorice ribbons. Makes 1 litre.

Thirty

Meringue Ghosts

2 egg whites   **⅛ teaspoon cream of tartar**
100g caster sugar   **¼ teaspoon vanilla essence**
1 large bag dark chocolate chips (around 72 chips)

Preheat the oven to 140°C/275°F/Gas 1. Line 2 baking trays with greaseproof paper, using a blob of meringue to secure. In a clean, dry bowl, whisk the egg whites and cream of tartar until thick. Gradually add the sugar, whisking all the time, until the meringue is stiff and glossy, then reduce the speed and whisk in the vanilla essence. Place the meringue in a piping bag and pipe around 24 ghost-shaped figures (around 10cm tall) direct onto the greaseproof paper. Put 3 chocolate chips on each face to form the eyes and mouth. Bake in the oven for an hour, then remove to cool before peeling away the greaseproof paper. Makes 24 ghosts.

Sticky Bonfire Pudding

100g pitted dates (chopped)   100g sultanas
1 orange (grated rind – squeeze the juice for the sauce)
1 teaspoon bicarbonate of soda   300ml boiling water
2 eggs   175g self-raising flour
For the sauce:
125g butter   75g light soft brown sugar
50g dark muscovado sugar   Juice from the orange

Preheat the oven to 180°C/350°F/Gas 4. Butter an ovenproof dish, around 20x30cm in size. Place the dates, sultanas, orange rind and bicarbonate of soda in a bowl and cover with the boiling water, leave for 10 minutes. In a separate bowl, break in the eggs, one a time, folding in a tablespoon of flour with each egg, then add the rest of the flour. Gradually add the soaked fruit (including the water) to the eggs and stir to combine. Pour into the greased ovenproof dish. Bake in the oven for 30 minutes, or until cooked (springy to touch). While the pudding is baking, make the sauce. Put all the sauce ingredients into a saucepan, stirring until the butter has melted and the sugar has dissolved. Simmer for 2 minutes, or until the sauce has thickened. When the pudding is cooked, remove from the oven and immediately poke holes in the top with a fork. Slowly pour over the sauce. Pop the pudding under a hot grill for a few minutes until the topping goes crunchy and sticky. Serve warm with a huge dollop of whipped cream. Serves 6.

Old Fashioned Apple Pie

For the pastry:
200g flour   110g butter (cubed)   Pinch salt   2 tablespoons cold water
For the filling:
700g cooking apples (peeled, cored and sliced)
2 tablespoons lemon juice   110g sugar   25g butter
1 level teaspoon ground cinnamon
Milk to glaze

Place the flour, butter and salt into a large bowl and rub with your fingertips until the mixture resembles fine breadcrumbs. Add the water to the mixture and using a cold knife stir until the dough binds together. Wrap the dough in clingfilm and chill for 30 minutes. Preheat the oven to 220°C/425°F/Gas 7. Meanwhile, simmer the apples with the lemon juice and a splash of water in a large pan for 10 minutes until soft. Stir through the sugar, butter and cinnamon then remove from the heat and leave to cool. Roll out half the pastry and line a 13cm pie dish. Put the apple mixture into the base, then roll out the remaining pastry to make a lid for the pie. Damp the edges of the pastry in the dish with a little cold water, cover with the lid, press the edges firmly together and crimp to seal. Brush the top of the pie with milk and bake in the oven for 25 minutes. Serve hot or cold with cream, ice cream or custard sauce. Serves 6.

Warming Whisky Baked Apples

200g mixed dried fruit   Splash lemon Juice
2 tablespoons thick cut marmalade
Pinch cinnamon   Dram whisky
4 tablespoons dark muscovado sugar (plus a little extra)
4 large cooking apples   Foil

Preheat the oven to 200°C/400°F/Gas 6. Mix the dried fruit, lemon juice, marmalade, cinnamon, whisky and sugar together in a large bowl and leave to marinate for 15 minutes. Core each apple (leaving the skin on) and fill the cavity with the dried fruit mixture. Sprinkle the top of each apple with a little extra sugar and any remaining mixture, then wrap securely in foil, with the open side on top but scrunched up. Keep upright and place on a baking tray. Bake in the oven for 30 minutes or until the apple is soft (check with a sharp knife). Carefully open the foil to retain the hot juices and serve with vanilla ice cream. Serves 4.

Triple Chocolate Brownies

**200g dark chocolate   125g butter (cubed)   110g caster sugar   2 eggs (beaten)
185g flour   100g milk chocolate chips   150g white chocolate chips**

Grease and line a 19cm square cake tin, and preheat the oven to 190°C/375°F/Gas 5. Break the dark chocolate into small pieces then add with the butter to a saucepan and stir over a very low heat until melted. Cool for 15 minutes, then add the sugar and eggs, followed by the flour. Fold through the chocolate chips and spread the mixture into the cake tin. Bake in the oven for 30 to 40 minutes until the brownies are firm to touch. Allow to cool, then turn out and cut into squares. Serve warm with whipped cream, or cold with hot custard. Makes around 10 brownies depending on size.

Easy Peanut Brittle

100g caster sugar   100g salted peanuts

Tip the sugar into a saucepan and place over a low heat. Shake the pan a little as the sugar starts to melt (but do not stir), until it turns a deep dark mahogany colour. Add the peanuts, stir and remove from the heat. Pour the hot mixture onto a baking tray lined with greaseproof paper. Once cold, break into shards with a toffee hammer or rolling pin and wrap each portion up in a paper cone. Serves 6.

Toffee Apples

8 green eating apples
8 wooden lolly sticks
400g golden caster sugar
100ml water
1 teaspoon vinegar
4 tablespoons golden syrup

Place the apples in a large bowl, then cover with some boiling water for a minute. Drain and dry thoroughly and twist off any stalks. Push a wooden lolly stick into the stalk end of each apple. Next, tip the sugar into a pan along with the water and cook over a medium heat for around 5 minutes until the sugar dissolves, then stir in the vinegar and syrup. Set a sugar thermometer in the pan and boil to 150°C or the 'hard crack' stage. Now, quickly (but carefully) dip and twist each apple in the hot toffee until covered, let any excess drip away, then place on a sheet of greaseproof paper to harden. Leave the toffee to cool before eating. Serves 8.

Witches Slices

300g self-raising flour
125g butter (cubed)
200g demerara sugar

150g dates (chopped)
1 egg (beaten)
125ml milk

Preheat the oven to 190°C/375°F/Gas 5 and grease and line a 20x30cm baking tin. Sift the flour into a mixing bowl, rub in the butter until the mixtures resembles fine breadcrumbs, then stir through the sugar. Place half the mixture in the baking tin, and press evenly to form a base. Next, add the dates to the remaining mixture, then stir in the egg and milk. Spread over the base layer. Bake in the oven for 30 minutes until lightly brown, then allow to cool before cutting into slices. Makes around 14 slices depending on size.

Cheesy Scones

225g self-raising flour
Pinch paprika
1 teaspoon baking powder
60g butter (cubed)

100g Cheddar cheese (grated)
Handful chives (finely chopped)
80ml milk, plus extra for glazing
Extra cheese (grated – for topping)

Preheat the oven to 200°C/400°F/Gas 6. In a bowl, sift together the flour, paprika and baking powder. Rub in the butter until the mixture resembles fine breadcrumbs. Next, fold through the grated cheese and chives. Make a well in the centre of the mixture and pour in enough milk to make a fairly soft but firm dough, adding additional milk as required. Flour a surface and roll out the dough to approximately 2cm thick. Cut out the scones with a medium cutter and then place on a greased baking tray. Glaze the top of each scone with milk and then sprinkle with a little cheese. Bake in the oven for 10 to 15 minutes or until golden brown and cooked through. Serves 6.

Witches Hats

Greaseproof paper   200g white chocolate
Black food colouring (powdered sort)
125g Rice Krispies   Icing sugar (for dusting)
Red liquorice string   Black icing pen
Star and moon shaped sweets

Cut the greaseproof paper into 6 circles, 20cm in diameter. Fold each circle in half, and then make a cone, taping the edge of the cone to secure. Break the chocolate into squares and melt in a bowl over a pan of boiling water. Add a good pinch of food colouring to the melted chocolate until it turns black. Immediately tip in the Rice Krispies and fold through the melted chocolate. Spoon the Rice Krispie mixture into the cones and place in the fridge to cool for 30 minutes. Remove from the fridge and carefully unwrap the cone paper. Dust the hat with a little icing sugar (using a tea strainer), then decorate by tying a bow of red liquorice string around the base. Using the black icing pen, stick on the sweets to decorate.

Chocolate Chip Cookie Caterpillar

1 tub white vanilla frosting
Green food colouring
1 large packet chocolate chip cookies
Pretzel sticks
1 packet small sweets (to create eyes and mouth)

In a small bowl, mix the frosting with around 10 drops of the food colouring. Spread the frosting on each chocolate chip cookie and place them all together to form a long sandwich, making sure the line has a slight 'S' curve to form the shape of a caterpillar. Snap each pretzel stick in half and insert downwards along the sides of the caterpillar to form legs. Decorate the front and back cookie with small sweets to form a face, using a little left over frosting to secure each sweet. Serve on a plate covered with a green napkin for a leafy effect.

Bonfire Toffee

75g golden syrup   **75g black treacle**   **150g light soft brown sugar**
75g butter (cubed)   **¼ teaspoon cream of tartar**

Line a 15x20cm baking tray with greaseproof paper. Place all the ingredients into a large heavy-based saucepan and cook over a medium heat until the butter has melted and the sugar has dissolved. Stir occasionally. Increase the heat and bring to the boil. Using a jam thermometer, check when the mixture reaches 140°C/285°F, take off the heat and pour carefully onto the lined tray. Let the toffee cool completely, then break into bite-sized shards with a toffee hammer or rolling pin. Serves 8.

Pumpkin Damper

Large pumpkin (peeled and chopped)
White pepper
1kg self-raising flour
60g butter (softened)

Preheat the oven to 220°C/425°F/Gas 7. Cook the pumpkin in simmering water for 20 minutes or until softened. Drain thoroughly and mash, adding a dash of white pepper then allow to cool. Sift the flour into a bowl and rub in the butter with your fingers to resemble fine breadcrumbs. Add the mashed pumpkin and a little water and mix into a sticky dough. Knead for a few minutes then cut the dough in half. Knead each portion for a further few minutes, then shape into 2 round loaves. Place on a greased baking tray, cut a cross on top of each damper and sift a little flour over both. Bake in the oven for 10 minutes, then reduce the heat to 180°C/350°F/Gas 4 and continue baking for a further 30 minutes until golden brown. Serve warm with lashings of butter.

Mulled Cider

**2 ltrs traditional cider   3 cloves   3 star anise   Nutmeg (grated)   1 cinnamon stick
1 vanilla pod (halved)   3 oranges (juice only)   1 pomegranate (juice and seeds)
4 tablespoons caster sugar (or slightly less to taste)**

Pour the cider into a large pan on a low heat and let it warm through for a few minutes. Add all the spices, juices and seeds and gently bring to the boil. Lower the heat and simmer for a further 5 minutes. Stir through the sugar until dissolved, then sieve and serve warm in large mugs.

Warming Hot Chocolate

**600ml milk   1 small pot double cream
150g dark chocolate (chopped)
To serve: sugar, squirty cream (from an aerosol), nutmeg (grated),
mini marshmallows, grated chocolate**

Pour the milk, double cream and chocolate into a pan. Bring to a gentle boil, whisking continuously until the chocolate has melted and the mixture is smooth. Serve in individual mugs, adding sugar to taste, then top with squirty cream and a choice of grated nutmeg, mini marshmallows or grated chocolate. Serves 4.

Rocket Fuel *(Bloody Mary)*

For each serving:
**2 ice cubes   vodka (double shot)   ½ lemon (juice only)
4 dashes Worcestershire sauce   3 dashes Tabasco sauce
150ml tomato juice   Salt and white pepper (to season)**

Place the ice into a tall glass and pour over the vodka. Next, add the lemon juice, Worcestershire sauce, Tabasco sauce and tomato juice. Stir well. Season to taste with salt and white pepper and serve immediately.

Worm Brew *(Non Alcholic Bloody Mary)*

For each serving:
**2 ice cubes   150ml tomato juice   Good splash lemon juice
2 dashes Worcestershire sauce   Dash Tabasco sauce   White pepper (to season)
A couple of gummy worm sweets**

Place the ice into a tall glass and pour over the tomato juice. Next, add the lemon juice, Worcestershire sauce and Tabasco sauce and stir well. Season to taste with white pepper. Balance the gummy worm sweets on the edge of the glass as if escaping from the brew. Serve immediately.

METRIC CONVERSIONS

The weights, measures and oven temperatures used in the preceding recipes can be easily converted to their imperial equivalents. The conversions listed below are only approximate, having been rounded up or down as may be appropriate.

Weights

Avoirdupois	Metric
1 oz.	just under 30 grams
4 oz. (¼ lb.)	app. 115 grams
8 oz. (½ lb.)	app. 230 grams
1 lb.	454 grams

Liquid Measures

Imperial	Metric
1 tablespoon (liquid only)	20 millilitres
1 fl. oz.	app. 30 millilitres
1 gill (¼ pt.)	app. 145 millilitres
½ pt.	app. 285 millilitres
1 pt.	app. 570 millilitres
1 qt.	app. 1.140 litres

Oven Temperatures

	°Celsius	°Fahrenheit	Gas Mark
Slow	140	275	1
	150	300	2
	170	325	3
Moderate	180	350	4
	190	375	5
	200	400	6
Hot	220	425	7
	230	450	8
	240	475	9

Flour as specified in these recipes refers to plain flour unless otherwise described.